# FIRST BOOK
## of
## PRACTICAL STUDIES

### for
### FRENCH HORN

*by*

ROBERT W. GETCHELL

## *Foreword*

This FIRST BOOK OF PRACTICAL STUDIES is designed to develop chord consciousness and to provide additional experience in the fundamental rhythms, key signatures, and articulations and to improve ACCURACY IN READING through the use of interesting and melodic studies. It may be used either to supplement or to follow any beginning method book and will serve as an ideal preparation for the slightly more advanced techniques to be found in the SECOND BOOK.

The following rhythms are introduced and developed in the FIRST BOOK:

> Eighth notes .................................... Etudes 13-31
> Dotted quarter notes ..................... Etudes 32-47
> Sixteenth notes ................................ Etudes 48-68
> Major scales (Diatonic & thirds) ................. Page 32

## 17

## 18

## 24

## 25

# 39

# 40

# 41

## 48

## 49

23

# 50

# 51

## 62

## 63

## 64

## 65

# MAJOR SCALES
## Diatonically and in Thirds